In memory of
Clarence E. Troyer
who cherished his experiences as tour guide, loved to tell the stories contained in this book and counted it a privilege to worship in this Historic Stone Church.

Voices from the Past
by Dorothy Troyer

Copyright © 2011
Dyeing Arts Books
Kentfield, California
www.dyeingarts.com
All rights reserved.

ISBN 978-0-9817244-3-0

Printed in the United States of America
by Lightning Source, Inc.

Voices from the Past

*A collection of
stories and testimonies about
the Community of Christ
Stone Church in Plano, Illinois*

by Dorothy Troyer

Table of Contents

Forward to the Past	2
HOW STONE CHURCH CAME TO BE	**4**
Please Build a Church	5
In the Beginning	7
EVERY STONE HAS A STORY	**8**
An Unusual Stone	9
Our Pulpit	11
More Than an Old Fashioned Desk	13
The Stone Church Basement	15
The Stone Church Pews	17
The Pipe Organ Story	19
JOSEPH SMITH III	**22**
Joseph Smith III As Plano Knew Him	23
The Importance of Every Step We Take – Joseph Smith III and the Well	27
A SITE OF HISTORY AND OF WORSHIP	**29**
Just Plano Hymns	30
The National Register	32
Stone Church International	34
The Awesome Power of Place	35
ADDITIONAL REFERENCES	**39**
Timeline	40
Pastors/Presiding Elders of the Plano Stone Church	41
Related Material	42

Forward to the Past

The Plano Stone Church is plain and austere, but certainly not ordinary. If they could speak, the very stones would have stories to tell. Stone Church is an historic site of the Community of Christ Church and is owned by the World Church headquarters of the denomination. It was the first church constructed after the Reorganization of the church under the leadership of Joseph Smith III. It is on the U.S. National Register of Historic Places because it is the oldest church building in continuous use in Kendall County of Illinois.

This book is dedicated to the men, women and children who worship regularly here in the Plano Stone Church. Every Sunday we sit in these hand hewn pews. We sing hymns written by people who were members of the Plano Congregation. The pulpit, the organ, the windows, the closets and even the basement have stories.

The stories in this book are those of the people who created and used this church building and its furnishing. Their testimonies permeate the atmosphere. To those who worshipped here in the past and for those worshipping here today, this is holy ground.

We have the rare blessing of calling this historic site our "church home" and the privilege of extending a warm welcome to all those who come as visitors. Buses deliver senior citizens and youth groups from all over the United States and Canada.

Although I wrote the pieces in this book that aren't otherwise attributed, they were inspired by history that I have read or heard over the years as a member of the Plano congregation. I had a lot of help from Betty Meier, our congregation's Historian and Donna Vickers, the Stone Church Tour Guide. As you read these stories and tell them to your children, you will come to love this place as much as the generations before us.

Dorothy Troyer
Pastor 1994 - 1998

How Stone Church Came to Be

This church has a story that is unique and inspiring. This section provides a few pieces of that story.

Please Build a Church

In 1844, Joseph Smith, Jr., founder, Prophet and President of the Church of Jesus Christ of Latter Day Saints, and his brother Hyrum were murdered in the Carthage, Illinois jail. Those who had followed their leadership were threatened. Some were persecuted for their beliefs. Left without leadership and frightened of the townspeople, the church members scattered in all directions. Some went west with Brigham Young. Nauvoo, where most of the church members had lived, soon became a ghost town. Isolated, the scattered Saints became disheartened and discouraged.

Then came the exciting news that Joseph Smith's son, Joseph III now age 27, was willing to assume the leadership of these scattered people, feeling that he had been called of God to do so. A meeting was held on April 6, 1860 in Amboy, IL where Joseph III was accepted as leader of what would now be called *The Reorganized Church of Jesus Christ of Latter Day Saints (RLDS)*.

It was a joyful occasion one year later when the first congregation of the RLDS Church was organized in Plano at the home of James and Anna Horton. Many of those who had been isolated, scattered, and discouraged were present that April day in 1861. Brother Horton became their first pastor.

Keeping a low profile, the "Saints" met in homes to worship and hold Sunday School classes. They lived and worked in Plano. The citizens of Plano soon recognized them as honest, hard working people and good neighbors.

Imagine how amazed these early members must have been when the citizens, who were not members of the church, came to them and said, "We would like you to build a church and we'll help you." The land on which the Stone Church now sits was donated by the Henning family, none of whom were members of the RLDS Church.

Work on the church began March 18, 1868. The stone came from a quarry on the Fox River, owned by Mr. Post. Footings of the building were outlined with a smooth-surfaced stone obtained in Aurora, as also were the corners, the arched windows and the doorways. Samuel Reynolds hauled the stone in his farm wagon.

Today the RLDS Church is called the Community of Christ. That building begun in 1868 is our Plano Stone Church. Members of the Henning family still live in the area. Donna Vicars, great, great granddaughter of Samuel Reynolds, is a church member and gives tours of our Stone Church.

In the Beginning

James Horton and his wife, Anna (Weeks), first heard the gospel in Pennsylvania. They moved west to Nauvoo, Illinois and lived there during the troublesome days that followed the death of Joseph Smith, Jr. In 1860, they moved to Plano with their children, seeking a place where they could follow their religious faith in peace.

On April 21, 1861 a small group of church members met in the Horton home to organize the first congregation of the RLDS Church. James Horton was elected first presiding elder/pastor of the branch. He served as pastor from 1861 thru 1863. Both he and his wife remained faithful and active members of the Plano Branch until their deaths; James in 1873 and Anna in 1874.

Their house located on US Route #34 was always pointed out during the walking tours until the summer of 2004 when it was razed by the State of Illinois to accommodate the widening of Route #34.

Every Stone has a Story

The Stone Church seems to have stories everywhere you look. This section provides some interesting information about how the things in our church came to be here.

An Unusual Stone

Above the double doors of the Stone Church entryway you will see an oblong plate of the same smooth-surfaced stone as you see on the church corners and over the arched windows and doorways. It is inscribed "Holiness to the Lord." Do you see anything unusual in the inscription? Look carefully.

Brother Wright, a painter, drew the motto and gave it to the stonecutter. In doing so he accidentally reversed the N in the word HOLINESS. The stonecutter inscribed the stone exactly like the drawing that had been given to him.

 One day a little girl and her mother stood in front of the church looking up at that stone. A member of the Plano Congregation happened to be walking by and stopped to see what they were looking at. The mother explained that her daughter's schoolteacher had given the class an assignment. They had to go to various places in Plano and look at things that were a bit unusual. One of the things on the teacher's list was the stone above the Stone Church doors. The assignment was to find out what was unusual about it and report back to the class.

In 2005 the stone was so badly worn that it could not be easily read. A duplicate stone was created to replace the worn one and it was agreed that the new stone should also have the reversed "N." The stone itself had become a famous, historical site among Plano school children. The original stone is in the foyer of the Stone Church.

Our Pulpit

On Sunday mornings members of the Plano congregation listen while announcements are made, scriptures are read, prayers are offered and a sermon is presented from a pulpit built in 1868 by members of the Stone Church Congregation. Every President/Prophet of the church, with the exception of Joseph Smith, Jr., has spoken from this pulpit. No other pulpit has ever been used in our Stone Church. It was originally made of two kinds of wood at a cost of $10. Later a wood base was added to raise the height. At first the pulpit was painted black, so the two kinds of wood were not visible. But in 1957-58 the pulpit was refinished to match the pews and the organ. Now, if you look carefully, you can see the two kinds of wood and the "new" base. So far, we haven't been able to name the two woods.

In 2010 the RLDS Church celebrated its 150th anniversary. As part of that celebration, the Stone Church's pulpit was shipped to Independence, Missouri to make an appearance at the 2010 World Conference.

The conference was called to order by President Stephen Veazy and the opening business of the conference was conducted from our pulpit. On Sunday evening after the close of the Business Session, our pulpit was taken to the Heritage Room where World Conference Delegates and visitors from many parts of the world could see it and touch it and even have their pictures taken standing behind or beside it.

Every Sunday we, as members of the Plano Community of Christ congregation, can see our pulpit, touch it and on occasion may even stand behind it. And a few have had their pictures taken with this historic pulpit. Arrangements can be made to do so. Please ask.

More Than an Old Fashioned Desk

This particular desk is in the library at Rogers Hall, next door to the Stone Church. It once belonged to Elijah Banta.

Elijah was a miner in Pennsylvania who studied the scriptures in every spare moment. From Pennsylvania he moved to Indiana to manage his father's farm. He became a state representative of Indiana and served as a Union soldier in the Civil War.

One day Elijah read a letter that appeared in a newspaper. It was about Joseph Smith III taking his place as President of the Reorganized Church of Jesus Christ of Latter Day Saints. That letter motivated Elijah and his wife, Emeline, to move to Sandwich, Illinois to be part of this interesting religious movement. In 1863 Elijah joined the church and became a counselor to Bishop Israel Rogers, the first Bishop of the Reorganization and the man for whom Rogers Hall is named. Today Elijah's desk is in the library of Rogers Hall.

In the early years of the Reorganization, General Conferences (now called World Conferences) were held in Plano. At the 1874 Conference a committee was chosen to design a church seal. The committee members were Joseph Smith III, Jason W. Briggs and Elijah Banta. Before that Conference ended, the committee submitted a design, a child standing by a lion and a lamb lying down to rest, was based on the scripture passage found in Isaiah 11:6. The motto was "Peace." A rendition of this seal, hand-carved by Richard Young, now hangs on the wall in the Stone Church. The very desk upon which it was probably designed is in the Rogers Hall Library.

When it is appropriate, go up and take a close look at the Church Seal carving. For a pattern, Richard was given a small picture cut out of an old Saints Herald. When he was not working he kept his work covered and asked his family not to look at it. At one point Richard confessed that he would not be able to make the letters around the edge stand up off the background and he would have to recess them. Yet, when the carving was finally complete and some of us were allowed to view it, the letters were not recessed. When asked why his reply was, "The Lord wouldn't allow me to do it that way."

The Stone Church Basement

On Sunday mornings, those who are involved in the worship service, meet in the basement to briefly go over the various parts of the service. The presider asks the Lord's blessing on that which has been prepared for the congregation. Then upstairs they go to walk down the middle aisle of the Stone Church to take their places in front.

Visitors who come for tours go to the basement to watch a 20-minute presentation giving a brief history of the Reorganization and how the Stone Church came to be built in Plano.

At one time there was a kitchen in the basement. Pot luck dinners and Sunday School classes were held there. But there wasn't always a basement.

In the mid 1930's Pastor Joseph M. Blakely led a group in the long laborious task of excavating the basement. Just imagine what it must have been like to fill buckets with dirt and carry them up a ladder to the outside of the building. Every able bodied person, even children, helped. Pastor Blakely was known to the children as Uncle Joe.

The citizens of Plano were always interested in the Stone Church happenings so in 1937 the following report was printed in the *Kendall County News:*

> **Basement Floor Laid in the Latter Day Saint Church**
> The people of the Latter Day Saint Church are very happy over the fact that the basement floor of their

church has been completed, and the basement can now be used for classrooms, social gatherings, etc. Mr. Howard Layton, Freeman Landers, and George Jepson poured the concrete for the floor last week.

The basement was dug out some time ago by volunteer help. An outside coal bin and rear entrance has been constructed at the west of the building. In the near future it is hoped to make further improvements in the basement and more fully complete it. But in the meantime it is a very decided asset to the building and will be much used during the coming winter months.

Steps to the basement were constructed in January 1938.

The Stone Church Pews

I was alone in the Stone Church. It was the middle of the week and I had brought some things to put in the small back room that had once held one of the church's furnaces. Now it was to be used as a nursery on Sunday mornings. I placed a padded rocking chair, draped a quilt over the back, arranged some books on the small table and organized a few toys. Then I walked down the middle aisle and sat in the second pew on the south side of the church. I thought about the people who had sat in the very same pew in the very same  spot and suddenly I realized that "those people" might have been my own grandparents. Ben and Sarah Sumption had heard the gospel preached on a street corner in England. They were young, newly married and filled with a sense of adventure. They decided to come to America to be part of this latter day religion. Their destination was Nauvoo, Illinois. But upon arriving they discovered that most of the people had headed west.

Disappointed, Ben and Sarah bought a small farm in Kewaunee, Illinois and began to raise their family. It was while living there that they were contacted by members of the Church of Jesus Christ of Latter Day Saints who had *not* gone west. Elders of this church were traveling around the state, on foot, searching for other members who had stayed in Illinois. My grandparents were told an amazing story about a young Joseph Smith III, an adult now and willing to be a leader for these scattered "Saints." He wanted to reaffirm the teachings of the church as they had been in the beginning of the organization. He rejected the teachings of polygamy and baptism for the dead. My grandparents joined this group, which became the Reorganized Church of Jesus Christ of Latter Day Saints and held General Conferences in this Stone Church.

It would have been a fair distance to travel by horse and buggy from Kewaunee to attend conferences in Plano. But Ben and Sarah had traveled much further to be a part of this exciting movement. They were still young and adventurous. They very well might have sat in this room, even the pew I sat in that day. I had not known my grandparents, but that day, sitting in this Stone Church, I felt a real kinship with them.

These pews were made by the hands of dedicated men. They are not comfortable pews. The great grandfather of Josephine Sherman, a woman in our congregation, helped construct these pews. One day Josephine asked him, "Grandfather, why didn't you make these pews more comfortable?" He replied, "These pews were made for listening, not for sitting." It takes a few Sundays for new members to find the pew that best fits their backs. It would be nice to know the names of people who once sat in the pew that is most comfortable for me. We might be related.

The Pipe Organ Story

Our Stone Church pipe organ has a name, a history, a price and a story of conversion to Christianity. Her name is Geneva and she came to live in the Stone Church in 1945.

Geneva began life as a theater organ in the Plano movie theater. We would hardly have recognized her then in her

black horseshoe shaped cabinet. Worldly music was her specialty. When the Plano Baptist Church purchased her, she got religion. Being somewhat of a disappointment to the Baptists, they sold her to the Plano congregation for $75. Installation cost another $250. It turned out the Baptists had good reason for their disappointment. Geneva was *not* dependable! Our congregation soon discovered that weather greatly affected the quality of her music. If it was cold, rainy or damp some of the keys did not respond. As time went on this problem became worse and Geneva in her unattractive black cabinet stood unused.

In 1956 Temple Organ Company from Independence, Missouri arrived in Plano with revival in mind. Geneva's relay (that had been in the basement) was re-installed into the console and electrified, thereby eliminating the earlier problems of weather. The black cabinet was replaced by a beautiful light wood church-like cabinet to match our pews. There was no doubt about it, Temple Organ Company had reached Geneva's heart. She was a new organ. She accepted Christianity and her music gives ministry in the Lord's name to this very day.

When Geneva was purchased in 1945 she was a 2 ½ rank organ. A rank is a graduated set of similar pipes that produce a distinct sound or tonal color. One year when John Hill of Century Pipe Organ Company was servicing the organ, he mentioned that additional ranks could be added. Betty Meier and her sister, Joan Gregory, decided to make that happen. Before the work could be done, Joan unexpectedly passed away. Betty went ahead with their plans and asked Mr. Hill to do the work. He completed the unfinished rank (the ½ of the 2½ original ranks) of "Salicional" and added the rank of "Celeste" on the swell in April 1999. Betty gave these upgrades as a memorial to dear relatives. In December 2001 a 21-note set of chimes was installed on the organ. This time Betty made the gift in memory of her sister, Joan.

The organ is now a four rank organ with chimes. All of the workings are in the enclosure at the front of the church. It is most interesting to open either side door and take a look at all the pipes and wind chests in there. Mr. Hill built a special ladder so he could reach up to the top.

We are grateful to those who purchased the Geneva organ, to Mr. Hill who loves coming to our historic church to keep her in good repair and to Betty Meier, whose gifts have greatly improved Geneva's abilities. Together, these people help us appreciate the saying, "God gave us music that we might pray without words."

Joseph Smith III

Joseph Smith III, sometimes referred to as "Young Joseph", was not only the leader of the church when the Stone Church was built. It was his home congregation for many years. These two pieces give us a little more insight into a man who played an important part in this church.

Joseph Smith III As Plano Knew Him
By Betty Meier – Written for the 150th anniversary of the Reorganization

In January 1866 Joseph Smith III and his family moved from Nauvoo, Illinois to Plano. Joseph's wife, Emmeline, became homesick for her family. Taking her baby son, she went back to Nauvoo for a visit. While in Nauvoo, the baby died. Three years later Emmeline passed away at the age of 31.

During Emmeline's illness Joseph had secured the services of Bertha Madison to care for Emmeline, the house, and their three young daughters. Bertha was from Mission, Illinois and a member of a devoted church family. After Emmeline's death, unkind and untrue gossip began about Joseph and Bertha. Joseph knew some change was required and made it a matter of prayer. After receiving an answer to his prayers he began to court Bertha and asked for her hand in marriage. Bertha and Joseph were married in Israel Rogers's home by Elijah Banta. Seven children were born to Bertha and Joseph in Plano. Two of those children later served as President/Prophet of the Reorganized Church of Jesus Christ of Latter Day Saints. They were Frederick Madison and Israel Alexander.

Joseph and Bertha lived in a home located on the corner of Dearborn and Hale Streets in Plano. It was the only house on the block when Joseph purchased it for $1,200. The house still stands at that corner and has always been well cared for by its owners.

Joseph III lived in Plano for fifteen years. During those years he served as President/Prophet of the church. For eleven of those years he also served as Pastor of the Plano Stone Church and Editor of The Herald, official publication of the church.

Joseph served the community of Plano as well as the church. He served two full terms (10 years) as the elected Justice of the Peace. He was the President of the Village Board, an office comparable to today's Mayor. In his spare time he served as captain of the Plano baseball team.

When the headquarters of the church moved to Lamoni, Iowa, the *Kendall County Record of Yorkville* published the following:

> "Elder Joseph Smith, the President of the *Reorganized Latter Day Saints*, took his final departure from Plano last Saturday night. Mr. Smith leaves Plano but carries the good will of Plano's citizens with him. He has

lived here for the past fifteen years and has always borne the reputation of a good citizen. Always to be found on the side of right, he maintained his position to the end, and goes to his future home with sad farewells and good wishes of his many friends."

Joseph did not forget his home in Plano. He returned many times and each time he visited he was a news item. For example:

"Elder Joseph Smith preached to a large audience, at the Stone Church Sunday morning and evening."

"Elder Joseph Smith's friends have been enjoying his presence among them again. He will always find hosts of warm friends in Plano."

In the Spring of 1865 the town of Plano held a memorial service for the slain President Abraham Lincoln. Joseph was invited to deliver the commemorative sermon. He also spoke at a memorial service for President James Garfield in the fall of 1881

Joseph Smith III, at a General Conference of the Church, counseled his people as follows:

"If the members of the church will gather together quietly here and there and live their religion, God will give them grace and favor with the people."

What a treasured history of the past we have. Joseph Smith III lived in this city and worshipped in this Stone Church. I imagine him walking through the swinging doors as he strode to the front to offer his ministry from our historic pulpit. He was here, walking among his people and the citizens of Plano, strolling the streets, visiting the shops and conducting his business at *The Herald*.

He lived his religion quietly, became involved in the community and won grace and favor with the people. What a rich heritage is ours.

The Importance of Every Step We Take – Joseph Smith III and the Well
Lachlan Mackay, Community of Christ Historic Sites Coordinator - Sermon given at Plano on November 15, 2009

As a child, Joseph Smith III lived with his parents on the east bank of the mighty Mississippi River in Nauvoo, Illinois. In his memoirs, Joseph recalled that next to their home was a shallow well which produced water of questionable quality. The Smith's decided to blast through the rock to deepen the well and improve its water. Young Joseph was very interested in this process. Following an explosion, he stepped outside to see the damage. Large rocks, thrown high into the air by the blast, were still on the way down. One of them, as it fell, nearly killed him. It brushed the brim of his hat on the way past and landed at his feet.

How different our story would be if Joseph had been one step faster. There would be no Reorganization, no Graceland University, no Fred M. Smith (or any of those who followed him in the presidency of the church until 1996), no Plano Stone Church, no Community of Christ Historic Sites Foundation, and no reason for us to be gathered here this week from around the world. How would your life be different but for one step not taken by a boy in 1840s Nauvoo?

Of course Joseph III wasn't injured those many years ago and so here we sit, inheritors of a legacy filled with wonderful and powerful stories and traditions. It is our shared sacred story that makes us into Community of Christ. As for the account of Joseph III and the well, it reminds us of the importance of every step we take as we play out our role in the sacred story.

My role in the story in some ways starts right here in Plano. In the early 1990s my mother worked for what was then known as Restoration Trail Foundation. I attended with her the ceremony in which the Stone Church was added to the National Register of Historic Places. While here, I had lunch with David Ettinger, then her boss, who invited me to apply for a historic sites internship in Nauvoo. Needing a way to kill some time while I applied for positions with the federal government, I accepted his offer. In preparation for my summer, I picked up a book on church history and began to read. Before I finished the book, I was captured by our story and as a result, I stand here eighteen years later as director of the church's historic sites. As a result, Plano is for me a sacred place in my personal sacred story.

A Site of History and of Worship

After 150 years, the Stone Church is both historic and current.

Just Plano Hymns

What do Mark Forscutt, David Smith, Frederick Smith, Joseph Smith III, Elbert Smith, Vida Smith and Audentia Anderson all have in common? They all lived in Plano at one time and they all wrote hymns that are in <u>Hymns of the Saints</u> hymnal published in 1981.

Some of these hymns are very familiar. *"You May Sing of the Beauty of Mountain and Dale,"* written by David Smith, is sometimes used as an opening hymn. At the close of the service perhaps you might sing, *"Lord Let Thy Blessing Rest in Peace,"* written by Joseph Smith III.

If there is a hymn sing and people are asked to request their favorite hymn, someone will ask for *"There's an Old, Old Path."* If it's sometime in December you may sing *"Silvery Star, Precious Star,"* an original Community of Christ Christmas Carol. Joseph Smith III wrote a long-time favorite, *"Tenderly, Tenderly Lead Thou Me On,"* a gentle hymn written by a tender-hearted leader.

Following is the list of 13 hymns written by these members.

Text or Tune by Mark Forscutt
- #   2   Met in Thy Sacred Name, O Lord - Text
- 112   Heavenly Father We Adore Thee - Text
- 24   Blest Be Thou O God of Israel – Tune
- 151   Every Good and Perfect Gift - Tune
- 436   Go Now Forth into the World - Tune

Text by Joseph Smith III
- 146 Tenderly, Tenderly, Lead Thou Me On
- 482 Let Us Breathe One Fervent Prayer
- 490 Lord Let Thy Blessing Rest

Text by David Smith
- 8 You May Sing of the Beauty
- 312 Let Us Pray for One Another

Others
- 158 There's an Old Old Path - text by Vida E. Smith, tune by Audentia Anderson
- 239 Silvery Star, Precious Star - text by Elbert A. Smith, tune by Audentia Anderson
- 316 Onward to Zion - text by Frederick M. Smith

Those who come for tours of our Stone Church will be invited to sing at least one of these hymns. Those of us who worship here every Sunday have the privilege of singing them more often. When you do sing them, listen carefully. You may hear voices from the past joining in.

The National Register

In the front of the Stone Church on the left as you face the front doors, there is a metal plaque indicating that the Stone Church is on the U.S. National Register of Historic

Sites. This plaque was placed there in 1991 by the United States Department of the Interior. It didn't just happen.

Ruth Wildermuth, Stone Church historian and Plano librarian, set out to prove that the Stone Church had the qualifications to be placed on this prestigious register. For several years she gathered and organized relevant information. She prepared a formal presentation and applied for permission to present her material to the proper authorities.

In 1990 Ruth traveled to Galena to present her case. Ruth argued that the Stone Church should be placed on the

National Register because our Stone Church is the oldest church in Kendall County in continuous use since it was built in 1868. Chapel on the Green, located in Yorkville, Illinois had made a similar request based on the same information. Ruth had to be very precise and very accurate in her facts. Much to our delight, she was successful.

The Plano congregation immediately began to plan a celebration. That celebration took place on April 20th and 21st, 1991. In the library in Rogers Hall there is an album of pictures taken at that event. Wallace B. Smith, President and Prophet of the church and grandson of Joseph Smith III, spoke from our historic pulpit. If you find that picture album, you may find pictures of people you know, even members of your own family.

Ruth Wildermuth served as Librarian for the Plano Library for 12 years. She was the Historian for the Plano Congregation and was the first woman in the Plano Community of Christ to be ordained to the priesthood

There are six other places in Plano on the National Register of Historic Places: Farnsworth Glass House, Plano Hotel, Chicago Burlington & Quincy Railroad Depot, Albert Sears Home and The Homestead (Lewis Steward's' home).

Stone Church International

The Plano Stone Church gets a wide variety of visitors; seniors, youth groups, people on vacation, and church members in search of their history. Some visitors come and go quickly while others linger. And some visits are extra special.

At the time Clarence Troyer was the Stone Church tour director, he received a phone call from Howard Sheehy, a member of the First Presidency. He asked if Clarence could lead a tour for him and two church members, a husband and wife from China. They had come for World Conference and were traveling around to see as many of the historic sites of the church as possible before they returned home.

Clarence met them at the church. In addition to the Stone Church, they did the Plano walking tour, which included Joseph Smith's home and the Herald Publishing House. As they walked together Clarence learned that both the husband and wife were elders in the church. Clarence was scheduled for major surgery in just a few days. When they concluded the tour, Clarence asked Brother Sheehy if it would be appropriate to ask these two elders to administer* to him. Brother Sheehy explained the request to the visitors and then cautioned Clarence that it would be a first for them. Neither of them had ever been asked to administer to anyone. But they were honored to be asked. So right here in our Stone Church two elders from China administered to a member of the Plano congregation in a never-to-be-forgotten experience.

*Administration is the act by ordained elders of laying hands on the head of a person in need and asking a special blessing.

The Awesome Power of Place
By Barb Walden, member of the Historic Sites Board
Presented at Plano Stone Church, November 15, 2009

Eight years ago, I found myself sitting in the basement of a museum in Cooperstown, New York with a baseball in hand – and experiencing a life changing moment.

While in graduate school, my husband Jody and I had the privilege of working at the National Baseball Hall of Fame and Museum. Jody worked in the education department where he had the terrible job of having to convince children that baseball is fun – can you imagine what a challenge that must have been like? While Jody was out enjoying the public, I was in the basement of the museum surrounded by historic artifacts. I was a collections manager and my job was to manage the literal baseball collection. Each day, I would arrive at work and research the history, condition, and significance of baseballs. After nearly six months of knowing my baseball shellac from my unconditioned rawhide, I opened a drawer and pulled out another ball. I remember looking at this particular ball and noticing that it had no unique markings, not a single autograph, just a brand name, stitching, and two numbers written in pencil: the number "6" and the number "1".

Whenever faced with a questionable ball, I would go to the old ledger books. There were several thick volume books that sat on the shelf and included bits of information about some of the older balls in the collection. As I searched, I found this particular ball's record number – as my finger traced the column with the number, I immediately ran my hand across the line to read the name of the ball. It read, "Roger Maris homerun ball

#61." I nearly passed out. My rush of excitement was soon replaced with overwhelming emotions. I sat there, with ball in hand, and just cried. As many of you know, Roger Maris' 61st homerun during the summer of 1961 changed history. It was a homerun race between Maris and his Yankee teammate, Mickey Mantle. Eventually, Roger Maris won the race and broke Babe Ruth's legendary record. It was an exciting event in American sports history, but I'm not totally certain it was worth crying over.

I left work that day and immediately watched the Billy Crystal movie "61," and of course called my father to celebrate what an extraordinary experience I had. When I hung up the phone with my father, I realized why I had been struck by a wave of emotion that day – it had absolutely nothing to do with Roger Maris, Babe Ruth, or the summer of 1961.

Baseball is a hallmark of the Walden family experience. Our summers were spent travelling from one park to the next. It didn't matter if it was minor league, major league, or little league – we loved the game. It seems that there were three things every Walden needed to know in life: 1. The ten commandments; 2. The three books of scripture; and 3. The line-up for the 1984 Detroit Tigers. My brothers and I had our favorite treats from the snack bar and had serious debates regarding the Dodger dog from LA vs. the foot-long from Detroit. It still feels like new life is birthed every spring around the time of spring training.

But as I hung up the phone with my father, I realized that for me, the Roger Maris ball represented the relationships forged with my parents and siblings while sitting in the bleachers of the ball parks. It was the excitement shared, the disappointment suffered, and the opportunity to grow closer as a family. The times spent at the games were a time of sharing as a family. It was in the long car rides to the field that we were able to get to know each other. The baseball represented the trust, love and loyalty we shared as a family unit.

As I stand here, behind this historic pulpit where so many of our historic leaders have once stood, I cannot help but feel a similar rush as what I experienced that day in the basement of the museum. What appears to be a traditional pulpit of the late 19th century is so much more to those of us who know the story behind this remarkable artifact. It represents the sacrifice of the early saints and the missionary zeal of Mark Forscutt and E.L. Kelley. It symbolizes the leadership of Joseph Smith III as he worked to forge a new organization that has lasted nearly two centuries and has impacted the lives of people all over the world.

In my experience as the site director at the Kirtland Temple, I was amazed to learn what the National Historic Landmark in Ohio represented to the visitors who traveled from all over the world to have an experience within its walls. For the pilgrims, the temple was not important because of the rubble stone construction or the beautiful windows. It was an important place because it represented the dreams and visions of a group of impoverished saints attempting the impossible task of creating sacred community. It inspires visitors to experience the breadth and depth of a God that inspired the Saints in the 1830s just as the Creator inspires us today.

I believe there is an immeasurable power of place. The opportunity to worship in this sacred place reminds us of the timelessness of our Creator and the strength of community found within these walls in the 1860s and 1870s when this place was the headquarters for a remarkable organization. Today, the power of this place continues to give meaning and life to those seeking a personal relationship with God. Here we experience anew what was felt in the days of old. This congregation has the awesome responsibility of not only preserving the past, both the stories and the materials culture, but also of inspiring the future generations. Our historic sites, including the historic Stone Church in Plano, are important; not because of the stories we tell, but because of the lessons these walls and pews hold; lessons so powerful, they will change our lives if we only listen. Such is the power of history!

Additional References

Timeline:

1830......... Joseph Smith, Jr. organizes the Church of Jesus Christ of Latter Day Saints in Palmyra New York.
1844......... Joseph Smith, Jr. killed in Carthage, Illinois
1860......... Joseph Smith III takes over leadership; church established as Reorganized Church of Jesus Christ of Latter Day Saints
1861......... Plano congregation organized in Horton home in Plano, Illionis
1866......... Joseph Smith III moved to Plano

1868......... Stone Church building began
1868......... Pulpit built
1872......... Reorganized Church incorporated
1874......... Church seal designed
1881......... Joseph Smith III moved to Lamoni, Iowa

1937......... Stone Church basement excavated
1938......... Steps to basement added
1945......... Pipe organ purchased
1957-58 ... Pulpit refinished

1991......... Placed on US National Register of Historic Places
1999......... Organ upgraded from 2 ½ rank to 4 rank
2001......... Added chimes to organ
2001......... Name of Reorganized Church of Jesus Christ of Latter Day Saints changed to "Community of Christ".
2005......... Stone replaced
2010......... Celebration of 150th anniversary of the Reorganization

Pastors/Presiding Elders of the Plano Stone Church Congregation

1861 (Apr.21)... Elder James Horton
1864 (May15) .. Elder Isaac Sheen
1866 (July 13) . President Joseph SmithIII
1871 (June13) .. Elder Mark H. Forscutt
1872 (Jan. 5) .... President Joseph SmithIII
1874 (Nov. 9) .. Elder Milton B. Oliver
1876 (May 7) ... Elder Frederick J. Pitt
1877 (June 4) ... President Joseph SmithIII
1881 (Sept. 30) Elder Wentworth Vickery
1896 (Feb. 5) ... Elder A. J. Keck
1897 (Feb. 10).. Elder Wentworth Vickery
1899 (Jan. 4) .... Elder A. J. Keck
1900 (Feb. 7) ... Elder Norman L. Blakely
1901 (Jan. 31) .. Elder Charles H. Burr
1902 (April 30). Elder Norman L. Blakely
1903 (Feb. 11).. Elder Francis M. Cooper
1905 (Oct. 4) .... Elder Henry Southwick
1907 (Feb. 18).. Elder Charles H. Burr
1907 (Dec. 31).. Elder Francis M. Cooper
1909 (May 10).. Elder Lester O. Wildermuth
1911 (Jan. 11)... Elder Eli M. Wildermuth
1913 (Jan. 1)..... Elder Joseph M. Blakely
1914 (Jan. 7)..... Elder Charles M. Burr
1915 (Jan)......... Elder Joseph M. Blakely (Elder Blakeley
                served as pastor for 25 years)
1940 (Fall)........ Elder Richard E.Wildermuth
1954 (Fall)........ Elder Gerald G. Blakely
1961 .... Elder Sumner Walker
1963.................. Elder Gerald G. Blakely
1963.................. Elder Sumner Walker
1964.................. Elder John Wahlgren
1965.................. Elder Lloyd Cleveland

1965.................. Elder Sumner Walker
1970.................. Elder Harley Pope
1972.................. Elder Terry Shelton
1973.................. Elder Sumner Walker
1975.................. Elder Terry Shelton
1979.................. Elder Sumner Walker
1980.................. Elder Terry Shelton
1981.................. Elder Sumner Walker
1982.................. Elder Joe Shelton
1984.................. Elder G. DuWayne Young
1990.................. Elder Dorothy Troyer
1994.................. Elder Clarence Troyer
1995.................. Elder Sandi Engelhorn
1996.................. Elder Dennis Ramer
2002.................. Elder Deborah Campbell
2004.................. Elders Jonathan Young & Janet Stoneking
2010.................. Elders Jonathan Young, Cynthia Ramer & Miranda Campbell

Related Material

More information about the Stone Church, its beginnings, and the people who were important in its formation can be found in the Stone Church library. Some of the items relevant to this book include:

Re-gathering of the Scattered Saints in Wisconsin and Illinois by Pearl Wilcox

Church History, Plano, 1861 – 1958 by Charles A. Reedy, Northeast Illinois District Historian

Acknowledgements

Thank you to those who helped make this book possible:

*Betty Meier and Donna Vicars
for providing historical information and photographs*

*Max Malone, Donna Vicars and Jon Young
for taking photographs of the current building*

*Joy Troyer
for editing and production assistance*

*Lachlan Mackay, Betty Meier, and Barb Walden
for giving permission to reprint their reflections*

*Plano Community of Christ congregation
for keeping the Stone Church alive and relevant*

www.ingramcontent.com/pod-product-compliance
Lightning Source LLC
Chambersburg PA
CBHW042049290426
44109CB00006B/156